Dedicated to all those who love truth.

The revolution has come...
Set on fire from the top
Let it burn swiftly.
Neither the branches, trunk, nor roots
will be endangered.
Only last years leaves and
the parasite bearded moss and orchids
will not be there
when the next spring brings
fresh growth and free standing flowers.

....

ONLY INTEGRITY IS GOING TO COUNT !
Human integrity is the uncompromising courage of self
determining whether or not to take initiatives,
support or cooperate with others in accord with all the
truth and nothing but the truth as it is conceived of by the
divine mind always available in each individual.

Whether humanity is to continue and comprehensively
prosper on Spaceship Earth depends entirely on the
integrity of the human individual and not on
the political and economic systems.

THE COSMIC QUESTION HAS BEEN ASKED:
ARE HUMANS A WORTHWHILE TO
UNIVERSE INVENTION ?

- R. Buckminster Fuller

Thor Janson

MAYA NATURE

Belize - Mexico - Guatemala
Honduras - El Salvador

With a Guide to Nature Reserves

Vista Publications
Guatemala, Central America

Published by Vista Publications
Apartado Postal 226-C, Metro 15
Guatemala, Central America
vhbookshop@intelnet.net.gt

*This book was reviewed for scientific accuracy
by biologist Peter Rockstroh, entomologist Dr.
Jack Schuster, botanist Dr. Elfriede Pöll and
speleologist Michael Shawcross.*

Book design by Manuel Corleto & Anne Brose.
Final production by The Watusi Alí Experience
with Jorge "Night Breed" Paz.

ISBN 0-9626221-8-4

First Printing
Printed in China

CONTENTS

Then they came together: Tepeu Hurricane, the Heart of Heaven, and Gucumatz, the Sovereign Plumed Serpent. There they conferred as the dawn of life was conceived. How should light and dawn be sown? Who is the provider, the nurturer?

Thus let it be done! Let the emptiness be filled! Let the water be removed! Let the earth appear and become solid! Let there be dawn in the sky and on the earth. But there shall be neither glory nor grandeur in our creation and design until the human being is made and man is formed. Thus they spoke.

Then the earth arose because of them. Earth! they said, and instantly it arose, like a cloud, like a mist, now forming, unfolding. Then the mountains were separated from the waters and suddenly the mountains grew.

From the Popol Vuh, sacred book of the Maya Quiche. One of only four Mayan texts to survive the Spanish Conquest.

INTRODUCTION

One of the most ecologically diverse regions on earth is found on the intercontinental land bridge running from the Isthmus of Tehuantepec in southern Mexico around through eastern Panama. The biogeographical realm of Central America is the crossroads where elements of two of the planet's great life zones, the *Nearctic* (North American) and *Neotropical* (South American) have intermingled. Changes in temperature and climate during glacial periods caused vast numbers of plant and animal species to migrate into the warmer equatorial regions. As they were funneled into the narrow isthmus of Central America, temperate species found themselves thrust into new relationships with the native tropical species. Evolutionary changes accelerated and new community structures emerged. Twelve thousand years ago, near the end of the Ice Age, glaciers reached as far south as St. Louis, Missouri, in the United States. Mastodons and giant ground sloths (*Megatherium*), the size of small elephants, roamed the mountains of Guatemala. Evidence suggests that the first humans arrived in Central America about this time, too. They were probably hunters following herds of large mammals which they relied upon for their sustenance. As the glaciers began to melt, a surge of icy water flooded into the Caribbean Sea, inundating the coastal lowlands and isolating many species on mountain tops, which had become islands. As the climate gradually warmed up again, many animals who prefer cooler conditions started to move north. Plants are often very sensitive to the temperature of their environment, and a change of just a few degrees may cause many varieties to move both in elevation and latitude. If we could compress ten thousand years into ten minutes, we would see the major movements which have taken place in plant communities. Pine forests which occurred along the coasts have moved up into the high mountains, while jungles similar in composition to those found in the Amazon basin have occupied the lowlands. Many species became extinct. Others were able to disperse into North and South America. Temperatures have remained relatively stable for thousands of years now, but the threat of global warming suggests that we may expect to see major changes in the composition of natural communities in the years to come.

What happened to the mastodons which were once common in Central America? We know without question that the aboriginal people used them for food. Some scientists believe that this and numerous other species were hunted into extinction in prehistoric times. Much still remains to be understood concerning the early evolution and movements of plants, animals, and humans. What we do know is that all these transformations and migrations have left Central America with one of the richest life systems on earth. Ancient mountain forests have nurtured the development of utterly unique endemic species. The horned guan (*Oreophasis derbianus*), a strange, turkey-sized bird instantly recognizable by the large, strawberry-red horn on its head, is found in the cloud forests of Guatemala and Chiapas and nowhere else on earth. Many unique kinds of plants are confined to a particular canyon or volcano.

The variety of distinct ecological zones found in the region is equally impressive. High in the Cuchumatanes Mountains of Guatemala, the visitor is met with a panorama reminiscent of the Rocky Mountains of Colorado. Dense coniferous forests give way to alpine meadows exuberant with wildflowers. Here mountain lions, coyotes, and ravens share habitat with jaguars and grey-headed taras. In the lowland jungles of southern Belize, the flora is 80 percent the same as that found in the Amazon Basin. This is the home of the kinkajou, the manatee, and the mot-mot bird. Five miles inland from the coast of Honduras, mountain ridges are constantly bathed in clouds, brought by the Caribbean trade winds. In these mysterious mist-enshrouded forests lives the mythical serpent bird, the resplendent quetzal.

This book you hold in your hand is intended to provide you with a general introduction to the wildlife of northern Central America. There are literally tens of thousands of different species to be found here. Nowhere on earth is the naturalist confronted with a more mind-boggling kaleidoscopic array of colors, scents, shapes, textures and unexpected surprises. Here you find photographs and information for identifying many species that the visiting explorer is likely to encounter as well as some of the more spectacular rare ones. Also included are descriptions of the best national parks and wildlife reserves of the region. For those interested in a more in-depth treatment of specific aspects of the natural world, field guides and other publications of interest are listed at the end of the book.

If you are attracted by the idea of exploring exotic tropical habitats and observing some of the world's most gorgeous creatures...then consider a tour through the Maya Realm.

ECOLOGICAL ZONES

The exceedingly varied types of soil and topography and diverse geological history of the country, ranging from ancient mountain masses connected with North America to relatively youthful volcanic areas, combined with marked altitudinal and climatic variations "hot desert to cold alpine regions" have given Guatemala the richest flora in all Central America with an estimated total of 8,000 species of vascular plants. Of this number, many are endemics confined to particular canyons and volcanos. Many genera and species of the United States and Mexico reach their southern limits of distribution in Guatemala, while a large number of South American genera and species either reach their northern limits of dispersal here or are unknown elsewhere from other parts of Central America. Orchidaceae, Leguminosae, and Compositae are especially prominent, and include hundreds of species, many of which are not found outside of Guatemala.

This is how Field Museum of Chicago botanists Standley and Steyermark described the heart of the Mayan Realm in their monumental work *Flora of Guatemala.* Tropical rain forests are located in a belt around the planet between the Tropic of Cancer (23° N) and the Tropic of Capricorn (23° S), the main limiting factor being temperature. Rain forests cannot exist where average temperature falls below 20 degrees centigrade. This temperature boundary is related to both latitude and altitude. Ecological zones occur because as altitude increases, temperature decreases, resulting in climatic conditions favoring different plant communities. The boundary for rain forest in northern Central America is reached at about 3,000 feet above sea level. At this elevation, there is a gradual transition into montane broad-leaf forest and higher up, mixed pine-oak forest. Along windswept mountain ridges the nearly permanent cold fog favors a ghostly pygmy forest where the trees are small and scraggly, covered with a profusion of orchids, bromeliads, and other epiphytes.

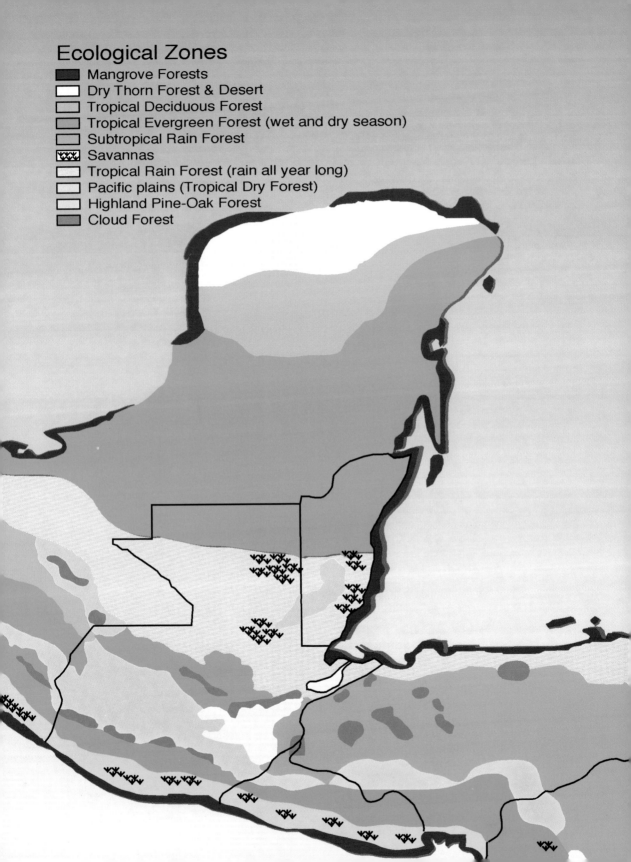

Ecological Zones

- Mangrove Forests
- Dry Thorn Forest & Desert
- Tropical Deciduous Forest
- Tropical Evergreen Forest (wet and dry season)
- Subtropical Rain Forest
- Savannas
- Tropical Rain Forest (rain all year long)
- Pacific plains (Tropical Dry Forest)
- Highland Pine-Oak Forest
- Cloud Forest

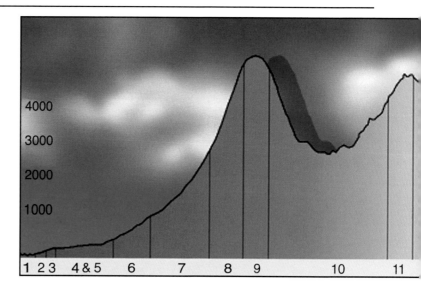

ECOLOGICAL PROFILE

If we made an expedition from the site of the proposed El Manchón National Park near the border between Guatemala and Mexico and followed a straight line northeast up to the Rio Lagarto Special Biosphere Reserve on the north coast of the Yucatan Peninsula, we would pass through some 20 distinct life zones. From the Pacific Coast we would go through the mangrove swamps, cross a wide belt of high coastal forest with pockets of savanna, and up into the mountains scaling the 13,000 foot peak of Tajumulco Volcano, the highest point in Central America. Then we go on through the springtime-like weather of the central highlands and up into the alpine habitats of the Cuchumatanes Mountains. From here we begin a gradual descent into the vast lowland forests of the Yucatan. Our route takes us through three biosphere reserves —Montes Azules, Maya, and Calakmul. As we move northward, rainfall diminishes and forests become drier and less exuberant. As we approach the end of our journey, we pass through wide belts of deciduous and dry thorn forests which are desertlike, hot, and arid. As we approach the northern coast, we once again find ourselves in the bug-infested mangrove swamps. Finally we reach the sand dunes and the blue waters of the Caribbean Sea.

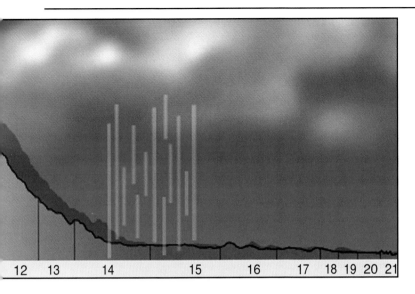

1.   Deep ocean trench to black volcanic sand beaches fringed with coconut palms.
2.   Mangrove-salt water swamp.
3.   Mangrove-zapote forests, brackish water lagoons, marshes, estuaries.
4.   Humid savanna with scattered pine trees.
5.   Pacific coast forest.
6.   Bocacosta (transitional zone)
7.   Tropical evergreen forest (marked wet and dry seasons).
8.   Cloud forest.
9.   Volcanic heights.
10.   Pine-oak-liquidambar forests.
11.   Alpine meadows.
12.   Pine-oak forests.
13.   Tropical evergreen forest (marked wet and dry seasons)
14.   Tropical rain forest (rain all year long)
15.   Tropical evergreen forest (marked wet and dry seasons)
16.   Tropical deciduous forest.
17.   Dry thorn forest.
18.   Mangrove-zapote forest, brackish lagoons, marshes, estuaries.
19.   Mangrove-salt water swamp.
20.   Ocean shore, white coral sand dunes and beaches fringed with coconut palms.
21.   Coral reef and sea grass communities.

THE CORAL REEF. In many respects the coral reef is the marine equivalent of the rain forest. They are both confined to the tropics, and it is here that the most exuberant diversity of life is found. The reef system running from the Yucatán Peninsula and along the entire coast of Belize is one of the longest barrier reefs in the world. Dozens of species of coral finger, brain, staghorn, and star coral provide habitat for large numbers of animals: lobsters, sea cucumbers, shrimp, sea stars, sponges, and a myriad of rainbow-colored tropical fish. A spotted trunk fish is seen in the foreground. (Photos Courtesy Carol Small-Kaplan).

Stoplight and rainbow parrot fish share the reef with blue damsel fish. Belize.

A brown surgeon and yellow pork-fish swim among a variety of coral species. Cozumel Island, Mexico.

THE MANGROVE SWAMP. Mangroves are comprised of a variety of salt-tolerant tree species and are the dominant form of vegetation along tropical coastlines, estuaries, and islands. Recognized by their long taproots, mangroves provide important refuge for nesting birds and a protected hatchery for many young fish. The tallest mangroves in the world are located within Encrucijada Ecological Reserve in Chiapas, Mexico.

FRESH WATER MARSH. This refuge for migratory and local waterfowl is located in south central Belize. In the distance towers Victoria Peak.

CARIBBEAN SHORE. Palm fringed, white coral sand beaches typify this stretch of the coast of Quintana Roo in Mexico. In the foreground the ancient Mayan ruins of Tulum.

CARIBBEAN COAST HABITAT. Punta Sal National Park, Honduras

RIO DULCE NATIONAL PARK. Tropical rain forest meets the aquatic habitat of one of Central America's Caribbean lowlands.

BRACKISH MARSH. Located several kilometers inland from the Pacific coast this aquatic habitat forms part of the Monterrico Nature Reserve in Guatemala.

THE PACIFIC COAST. This beautiful section of El Salvador's coastline was once important for its production of balsam tree extract.

TROPICAL RAIN FOREST. Ecotourists explore the lagoons and waterways of the Chocon-Machacas Manatee Reserve in Guatemala (easy on the smoke there boys!).

TROPICAL RAIN FOREST. The cool mountain water of the Rio Tulija flows through the forest of Agua Azul Nature Reserve,Chiapas, Mexico. The rain forest ecology is the result of abundant rainfall year round, combined with high temperatures. Constant warm, wet conditions have allowed for slow, uninterrupted evolution to take place and provide for the emergence of forests of remarkable structural complexity.

COASTAL HABITAT. Bacalar Lagoon, Quintana Roo, Mexico. The beautiful bright blue color of the ocean is indicative of the coral reefs which cover much of the coastal shelf along the Yucatan Peninsula. White coral sand beaches with coconut palms and mangrove swamps are quintessential tropical shore habitats.

TROPICAL EVERGREEN FOREST. As you sit atop one of the pyramids at Tikal National Park surveying the endless area of green, it is difficult to imagine that during the Mayan Classic Period (400-900 A.D.), this whole region was converted to agriculture, agroforestry, and silviculture. These forests are not as 'pristine' as they seem, and their actual species composition may be largely due to Mayan silviculture.

TROPICAL EVERGREEN FOREST. Dozens of tree species employ huge buttress-roots to provide extra support in the shallow soil typical of tropical forests. Tikal National Park, El Peten Province, Guatemala.

IXOBEL CAVE. Located near the settlement of Poptun, El Peten Province, Guatemala (color filters were used to create this photograph).

IXOBEL CAVE.

CAVE SPIDER. *Amblypigidae* species.

CAVE HABITATS. Extensive limestone geologic formations extend from northern Guatemala and Belize up through the Yucatán Península. Here some of the world's largest cave systems have been discovered. Caves provide habitat for a variety of unusual creatures including blind catfish, crickets, spiders, and dozens of species of bats. Occasionally a jaguar or other terrestrial mammal will take up residence near the entrance. Cave exploration, especially cave diving, can be very dangerous and should only be attempted with the assistance of expert guides.

TOK'BE HA' (hidden water) CAVE. Located near Ixcacel Beach.Quintana Roo, Mexico.

CENTRAL HIGHLANDS. Lake Atitlan National Park. Guatemala.

ALPINE HABITAT. High in Guatemala's Cuchumatanes Mountains route 9-N, one of the highest roads in Central America, weaves through cool pine forests.

CENTRAL HIGHLANDS. The Salcaja Valley near the regional capital of Quetzaltenango, Guatemala, Pine-oak forests predominate.

QUASI-PARAMO HABITAT. The rocky terrain of this high plateau in the Cuchumatanes Mountains of Guatemala was sculpted by glaciers during the last ice age. Tussock grasses and a variety of succulents, including agaves and cactus, are abundant.

CLOUD FOREST. High on mountain ridges and near the top of volcanoes lie cloud - enshrouded forests bathed in perpetual mist. The Indians call the constant misting rain "chippy-chippy". Sierra de las Minas Biosphere Reserve, Guatemala.

CLOUD FOREST. Trees are heavily laden with epiphytes, mosses, lichens, and bromeliads. Mario Dary Quetzal Reserve, Guatemala.

CLOUD FOREST. Giant tree-ferns *Alsophila salvinii* lend a prehistoric feeling to this habitat. Mario Dary Quetzal Reserve, Guatemala.

CLOUD FOREST. The forest plays an essential role in regulating the water cycle. The vegetation and soil act as a sponge, storing up water and releasing it gradually into the rivers. Following the destruction of the forest, droughts and floods become the norm.

HIGHLAND BROADLEAF FOREST.
Montecristo National Park, El Salvador.

CLOUD FOREST. La Tigra National Park,
Honduras. The cool, moist conditions found
in montane cloud forests stimulate the
development of lush vegetation. Trees are
typically covered in a variety of epiphytic
orchids, bromeliads, and mosses. Unique,
endemic species are common.

EPIPHITIC PLANTS. A large
variety of vines, succulents,
orchids, and other plants rely
upon already established trees
to gain a place in the sun.

PACAYA VOLCANO NATIONAL PARK, Guatemala, Central America is located on the edge of the Pacific "ring of fire". It is here where several of Earth's major tectonic plates crash into each other. Frequent tremors and numerous active volcanoes attest to the region's geological instability.

TROPICAL RAIN FOREST. Palenque Ruins National Park, Chiapas, Mexico. Twelve hundred years ago nearly all of the original rain forest had been cleared by the Maya. What we see today is actually advanced secondary growth.

TROPICAL DECIDUOUS FOREST. El Sumidero Canyon National Park, Chiapas, Mexico. From the rim of this tremendous canyon the visitor is given a spectacular view of the Santo Domingo River more than three thousand feet below. According to legend, hundreds of Indian warriors were surrounded here by the Spanish conquistadores, but rather than submit, they hurled themselves into the abyss.

SAVANNA. A combination of climatic factors and occasional burning produce extensive savannas in central Belize. The gritty soil is covered by a variety of grasses and shrubs with small stands of Caribbean pine and palmetto here and there.

WILDFLOWERS

In the region covered by this book literally thousands upon thousands of wildflowers flourish in every habitat from hot steamy coastal swamp all the way up to cool alpine meadows. The following photographs present a mere sampling of the incredible variety of color, texture, and form which await the tropical explorer.

TERRESTRIAL ORCHID. *Sobralia macrantha*. Highlands.

ORCHID. *Laelia digbyana*. Lowlands.

WILDFLOWER. *Erynigium sp.* Lowlands.

WILDFLOWER. *Mimosa albida*. Highlands.

'WHITE NUN' ORCHID. *Lycaste skinneri*   WILDFLOWER.
var. Alba. Cloud Forest.

EPIPHYTIC CACTUS. Genera: *Epiphillium*. Cloud forest.

CACTUS. Genera: *Rhipsalis*.   WILDFLOWER.   SUCCULENT FLOWER.
Lowlands to mid-elevation.   *Tradescantia crassifolia*.   *Hylocereus undatus*.
                                  Lowlands.   Highlands.

YELLOW TABEBUIA. *Tabebuia chrysantha*. Lowlands.
CONFETTI FLOWER. *Antigounon leptopus*. Lowlands.

MINIATURE ORCHID Genera: *Pleurothallis.*Cloud forest.
ORCHID *Notylia bicolor*. Highlands.

MINIATURE ORCHID. *Pleurothallis restrepia*. Cloud forest.

WILDFLOWER. Calliandra species. Lowlands.

WATER LILY. *Nymphea ampla*. Lowlands.

ORCHID. *Cattleya guatemalensis*. Cloud forest.

Rain forest in southern Belize is put to the torch to provide land for the production of oranges. Juice concentrate is exported to North America and Europe.

In the photograph we are seeing a section of the Maya Biosphere Reserve which has been recently cleared in defiance of Guatemalan law.

THE HAMBURGER CONNECTION

Cattle ranching is a primary cause of rain forest destruction in Central and South America. Since 1960, more than 25 percent of the forests in Central America have been cleared to create pasture land for grazing cattle. The beef produced is exported and used in the fast foods industries of North America and Europe. For every quarter pound hamburger 55 square feet of rain forest is destroyed.

It is a common misconception that rain forests are "the lungs of the world," providing much of the planet's oxygen. The truth is that the animals and microorganisms use up almost all the oxygen the trees produce. Rain forests do function as planetary air conditioners. Every day enormous amounts of water evaporates from the trees creating clouds. Clouds in turn reflect sunlight keeping the planetary surface cool and comfortable. By cutting down the forest we increase global greenhouse gases (carbon dioxide) while decreasing the protective cloud cover.

Rain forest colonist. It is important to remember that these hardworking farmers are only trying to survive. Unless given alternatives they have no choice but to continue cutting the forest.

INVERTEBRATES

Approximately 95 percent of the earth's animal species are included in the enormous taxonomic group *Invertebrata*, which includes all creatures without backbones, from amoebas to worms, insects and arachnids, to crabs, shrimps, and snails. The estimated number of the planet's total species has been revised numerous times in recent years due to the discovery of a multitude of new types of insects found in the tropical rain forest. Twenty years ago some taxonomists spoke of a probable five million total species, and this was thought by many to be an exaggeration. Today you hear numbers like 30, 50, even 60 million species. These revisions are due to the amazing results coming out of recent research in the rain forest canopy. Scientists have also discovered that many insects are specialized pollinators essential to the survival of particular plant species. This increases our understanding of why it will be impossible to ever recreate a tropical rain forest. The web of essential interrelationships between such vast numbers of organisms is so complex that only Nature with unlimited time at Her disposal could ever recreate similar diversity and complexity, all functioning together in harmony. So let's do what we can to save the forests. Because when they're gone, they're gone! And remember, Nature and Planet Earth are not endangered by present human folly. Nature has all the time in the world to put things right again. Humans are the ones putting their own future at risk by destroying the natural ecology and disturbing the balance which has provided us with a benign and nurturing environment for millions of years. It is urgent that we again learn to love and respect our Mother, the Earth.

BUTTERFLY. Family: *Nymphalidae.*

SEA ANEMONE. Class: *Anthozoa*. On the reef, numerous primitive animals, such as sponges, corals, and anemones have opted to sacrifice mobility and allow the ocean currents to bring food to them.

LAND HERMIT CRAB. *Coenobita clypeatus.* This little crab adopts a variety of snail shells as its protection against predators. Most active at night, it spends its days in burrows or concealed among the mangrove roots.

SCORPION. Family: *Centruridae*. Scorpions use their lobsterlike claws to capture prey. The stinger is employed to subdue prey and for defense.Like most arachnids, the scorpion uses "external digestion" whereby the victim is injected with digestive enzymes. After waiting for a while the scorpion sucks up the dissolved internal organs with specialized mouth parts.

LEAF-CUTTER ANTS. Family: *Formicidae.* These foragers create semipermanent trail systems through the forest leading from their nest to trees which they defoliate. The leaf matter is used as growth medium in subterranean mushroom gardens which provide the ants with food.

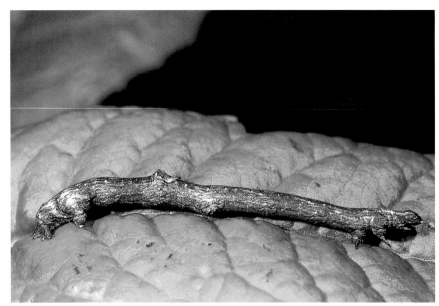

CATERPILLAR. Family: *Geometridae*.Perfect camouflage protects the immature larva from the onslaught of foraging birds. When disturbed these small inchworms stand up at a forty-five degree angle, making them look exactly like a twig protruding from a branch.

GIANT CENTIPEDE. Family: *Scolopendra*. Not to be confused with the harmless millipede, this aggressive carnivore is equipped with two poison-exuding fangs with which it subdues its prey. It spends most of its time underneath the leaf litter on the forest floor.

GIANT MILLEPEDE. Class: *Diplopoda*.This harmless forager is often seen along the highland trails. When threatened it rolls up into a tight ball. If molested it can spray a stream of poison containing hydrogen cyanide from its hindgut.

MANTIS. Family: *Mantidae*.Many species of mantis are found throughout the region. They come in an amazing variety of colors and forms. Many are highly mimetic, exhibiting perfect camouflage. After mating, the female typically eats the male. Mantis have great potential as biological pest control as they are voracious eaters of many insects that adversely affect human food crops.

ORB-WEAVER SPIDER.
Family: *Araneidae.* A
relatively large spider
which spins an equally
large and conspicuous
web.

ORB-WEAVER SPIDER.
(detail)

MINIATURE CRAB SPIDER. Family: *Apidae*. This tiny spider assumes the color of the flower it is on. Perfectly camouflaged it lays in wait for nectar seeking bees.

TIGER TARANTULA. Family: *Theraphosidae*. Although mildly poisonous and scary looking, tarantulas seldom bite unless tormented. A nocturnal predator.

LEAF BEETLE. Family: *Chrysomlidae.* This beautiful insect is a member of one of the most diverse beetle families in the tropics with literally thousands of related species. As forests are cleared for agriculture, some of these beetles become serious pests.

JUMPING SPIDER. Family: *Salticidae.* This is a highly diverse group of spiders, with thousands of species identified. They range in size from minute to over an inch in length. They are highly specialized hunters and stalkers. Their two pairs of hindlegs are extremely strong, allowing them to jump ten to twenty times their own body length, pouncing upon unsuspecting prey.

BUTTERFLY. Family: *Nymphalidae.* This beautiful butterfly exhibits the coloration typical of its family - flashy, bright colors on the upper wings and cryptic coloration underneath - giving it near invisibility when resting on a tree branch. It feeds on rotten fruit.

CONE-HEADED GRASSHOPPER. Family: *Tettigoniidae.* In Mexico some species of this family are fried up and served as a delicacy by the natives. They are said to taste something like stale, crunchy peanuts.

BUTTERFLY. Family: *Nymphalidae*.

CATERPILLAR. *Pseudosphinx tetrio.*

BUTTERFLY. *Nymphalis antiope.*Common in the highlands. This species, more common in the temperate Neotropics, ranges into tropical Mexico and Central America via the mountain ranges spanning the continent.

SWALLOW-TAIL BUTTERFLY. Family: *Papilionidae.*

BUTTERFLY. Family: *Nymphalidae.* These highly territorial members of the genus Hamadryas are known as "clicking" butterflies. Males sit head down on a tree trunk and whenever an intruder appears, they fly out at them making an audible clicking sound.

KATYDID. Family: *Tettigoniidae.* You can tell that this is a female because of the tail-like protrusion which is actually an ovipositor. The insect's ear is located on the foreleg.

MORPHO BUTTERFLY. Family: *Morphidae.* Female laying eggs.

MORPHO CATERPILLARS. Metamorphosis is completed inside the chrysalis.

MORPHO BUTTERFLY. Family : *Morphidae.*

Newly emerged butterfly dries its wings before taking flight

One of the most unforgettable images from the rain forest is that of large iridescent Morpho butterflies gracefully flying over the undergrowth. Their intense blue coloration stands out like a neon light against the muted green backdrop.

REPTILES AND AMPHIBIANS

Scientists have identified some 150 species of amphibians and 250 species of reptiles in northern Central America. They occupy the most diverse variety of ecological niches, from desert-living beaded lizards to aquatic toads and crocodiles, to arboreal vipers and tree frogs, to little salamanders living beneath the leaves and fallen trunks on the forest floor. As you swing in your hammock listening to the night sounds of the rain forest, the buzz of mosquitoes and the chirping of crickets invariably will be accompanied by the songs of nocturnal toads and frogs. All amphibians share certain characteristics. They are born from gelatinous eggs laid in or near water, pass through an aquatic larval stage at which time they breathe with gills (tadpoles), and finally undergo a metamorphosis to assume their adult form. The most abundant and diverse group of amphibians are the frogs and toads. The principal difference between reptiles and amphibians is that reptiles do not pass through a larval stage, and they are covered with scales which protect them from desiccation and allow them to live in dryer areas.

Most people visiting the rain forest for the first time are worried about poisonous snakes. Of the more than 125 snakes found in the region covered by this book, only 22 are dangerous. Many of these species are superbly camouflaged, which not only allows them to elude predators, but helps them in creeping up on prey. Others prefer to alert potential enemies of their poisonous status by exhibiting bright colors, as seen in coral snakes and golden eyelash vipers. One of your first encounters with tropical lizards may come when you hear strange chirping sounds in your hotel room at night. It is not uncommon in the tropical lowlands to share your room with a few geckos. These lovely little lizards are equipped with suctionlike scales on their feet which allow them to scurry all over the walls and ceilings as they hunt for insects. The fact that they help eliminate cockroaches and other pests makes them welcome residents in most homes.

RED-EYED TREE FROG. *Agalychinis callydryas.* By far the most abundant and diverse group of amphibians in Central America are the anurans which include frogs, tree frogs, and toads. Amphibians are animals that require an aquatic environment in order to reproduce. A female tree frog attaches her eggs to a leaf while the male fertilizes them. After five days the eggs hatch and the larvae drop off into a pond. During this phase the larvae, also called tadpoles, breathe through external gill tufts. When the larvae pass through metamorphosis the gills are lost, and the adult frog now breathes air through lungs. Most of its life is spent high up in the forest canopy. (Photo by Carol Farneti - Foster)

BANDED BASILIK LIZARD. *Bassilicus vittatus*. Juvenile female. Known as the "Jesus Christ lizards" for their remarkable ability to run on the top of water, these reptiles are common residents of gallery forests.

TREE FROG. *Smilisca baudini*. Common in the lowland rain forest. Suction cups for finger pads give tree frogs the ability to leap from one wet leaf to another with incredible agility.

TOAD. *Bufo valliceps*. This rather large toad is very common in the lowlands.

CROCODILE. *Crocodilus moreletti.* One of three crocodilians found in the region, these reptiles can easily exceed four meters in length. This species is endangered and exists exclusively in southern Mexico, Belize, and Guatemala. Can be dangerous.

BEADED LIZARD. *Heloderma horridum avarezi*. The only poisonous lizard in the region, these usually tranquil animals prefer hot, arid environments.

CROCODILE LIZARD. Genus: *Abronia.* Arboreal lizards which are most commonly found in the rain forest canopy where they spend their days hunting small insects in and around bromeliads. They are viviparous and are equipped with prehensile tails.

LOGGERHEAD SEA TURTLE.
Caretta caretta. This extremely rare two-
headed turtle was found at the Ixcacel
Turtle Refuge, Quintana Roo, Mexico.

Baby sea turtles are given a helping hand at
hatcheries located on both coasts.

LOGGERHEAD SEA TURTLES. *Caretta caretta*. Little is known about the natural history
of these marine reptiles. Most of their lives are spent swimming in the open ocean.
Females return to the same beach where they were born to lay eggs. This is the only time
they leave the water.

BANDED BASILIK LIZARD. *Bassiliscus vittatus*. Common in the hot lowlands. This adult male exhibits the sexual dymorphism typical of the species. Notice the large nuchal crest and dewlap which are absent from the female.

RIVER TURTLES. *Trachemys cripta.* Known locally as the "jicotea" these are among the most common fresh water turtles found in the region.

SPINY LIZARD. *Phrynosoma asio.* This small terrestrial reptile has chameleon-like camouflage which allows it to blend in with its surroundings.

GREEN AND BLACK IGUANAS. *Iguana iguana* and *Ctenosaura similis.*. These two iguana species inhabit tropical lowlands and are usually found in trees along rivers. The large green iguana is vegetarian in habit and can reach nearly two meters in length. The smaller black iguana is more omnivorous and will eat mice, baby birds, and insects as well as fruits and leaves.

VINE SNAKE. *Oxybelis fulgidus.* This beautiful snake reaches nearly two meters in length. It is arboreal and feeds on small lizards.

BOA CONSTRICTOR. *Boa constrictor imperator*. Common in undisturbed lowland forest, often reaching four meters in length, boas feed primarily on rodents and other small mammals. Although not poisonous, these snakes can be quite aggressive when disturbed and certainly capable of giving the molester a nasty bite. Natives of Central America hunt this snake for food and for its beautiful skin.

HOG-NOSED PITVIPER. *Porthidium ophryomegas*. Low and mid-elevation forests of Guatemala and El Salvador.

VINE SNAKE. *Elaphe flavirufa*. Low and mid-elevations forests. These completely harmless snakes reach more than one meter in length and are considered very beneficial to have around because of their voracious appetite for rats and mice.

SHULVA or CINCUATE. *Pituophis lineaticollis*. This large but harmless snake is found in the cold highlands where it hunts for mice and rats. It is widely, but absurdly, accused of sucking milk from cows and women.

GOLDEN EYELASH VIPERS. *Bothrops schegelii*. This small arboreal pit viper is considered to possess very potent venom. It lives in trees and bushes in mid-elevation forests where it hunts for mice and lizards.

FALSE CORAL SNAKE. *Lampropeltis triangulum*. Often confused with the true coral snake, this beautiful and harmless snake is found in both jungles and mountainous regions.

TRUE CORAL SNAKE. *Micrurus negrocinctus*. These highly poisonous snakes are largely nocturnal and usually live under the humid leaf layer on the forest floor where they hunt small salamanders and lizards.

TROPICAL RATTLESNAKE. *Crotalus durissus*. Known locally as the "royal viper," this is one of the most venomous snakes in the region. They reach a length of two meters or more. Rattlesnakes hunt rats, rabbits, and other small mammals. Widely distributed.

TROPICAL RATTLESNAKE. (Detail). TROPICAL RATTLESNAKE. (Detail).

GUATEMALA PALM VIPER. *Bothriechis bicolor*. This arboreal viper should not be confused with other similar-looking vine snakes. Its triangular head attests to the fact that it is indeed a viper and quite poisonous. Inhabits mid-elevation forests.

FER-DE-LANCE. *Bothrops asper*. Known locally as the "barba amarilla" or "yellow beard" this large snake is the most feared viper in the region. It is quite common in the low-land jungles and has a reputation of being aggressive. If you see one give it a wide berth.

CANTIL. *Agkistrodon bilineatus*. This semi-aquatic viper lives near streams and swamps where it hunts fish and rats. It is highly agile and nervous in behavior and is completely at home in the water. It may remain there for hours with only its head exposed waiting for unsuspecting prey.

VIPER. *Porthidium godmani*. Chiapas highlands color variation. Most pit vipers prefer warm lowlands, but this species is found only in high, cold mountainous regions in both coniferous and broad-leaf cloud forests. Normally reaching only half a meter in length, this small viper hides in the leaf litter on the forest floor.

VIPER. *Porthidium godmani*. Guatemala highlands color variation. Probably the most abundant viper found in the mountains of Guatemala. Its coloration makes it hard to see on the dimly-lit forest floor. Generally speaking, they only bite when stepped on.

GREEN EYELASH VIPER. *Bothrops schlegelii.* This small arboreal viper is perfectly camouflaged which also makes it particularly dangerous because it is so hard to see it in the foliage. Its venom contains powerful neurotoxins. Most abundant in mid-elevation forests.

BIRDS

In northern Central America some 800 species of birds have been identified. Of these, approximately 150 are migratory, flying down each autumn from North America. Many migrants, such as hummingbirds, tanagers, orioles, *Tyrannid* flycatchers, and wood warblers, are essentially tropical. They originally evolved in the neotropics and only later extended their range into North America in search of new feeding areas and better nesting grounds. In winter they share the forests and marshlands with avian families which are confined to the tropics, such as cotingas, manakins, toucans, antbirds, and woodcreepers. The feathered king of the rain forest is undisputedly the spectacular harpy eagle, the largest eagle in the world. Its main foods are monkeys and sloths, which it swoops in on and captures, using its tremendously powerful talons. The harpy eagle sits at the top of the food chain, and its presence in a forest is a good indicator of the ecosystem's overall health. It has been sighted in recent times in all of the huge biosphere reserves of the region. Nevertheless, very few people have ever had the thrill of seeing one. The emerald lord of the cloud forest is the elusive resplendent quetzal. Increasingly rare, this bird can best be seen if you spend a few days at one of the cloud forest reserves listed at the end of the book.

Visitors new to tropical forests often exclaim, "Where are all the birds?" The fact is that tropical species are furtive and surreptitious in behavior. They are there, but you have to look a little harder to see them than in other areas. Many times I have spent hours searching the forest to photograph a particular bird without ever a glimpse of one. And then, when I'm just about to give up, my eye catches a slight movement above me. There, sitting silently watching, is a resplendent quetzal, not more than 30 feet away. The quetzal's green color and serpentine tail blend in perfectly with the profusion of epiphytes and dangling mosses covering the trees. If you are lucky, you may encounter a tree bearing ripe fruit. Then you may see many different species congregating and eating in the same location. Successful birding in the tropics requires patience, keen eyesight, and a good knowledge of the species' natural history.

RESPLENDENT QUETZAL (male). *Pharomachrus mocinno.* The emerald serpent bird of the cloud forest.

ANHINGA (female). *Anhinga anhinga*. Distinguished from cormorants by their pointed rather than hooked bill, anhingas frequent lakes, rivers, and lagoons where they hunt fish.

GREY-NECKED WOOD-RAIL. *Aramides cajanea*. Forages for frogs and small insects in mangrove swamps and coastal lagoons. Seen less frequently around highland lakes.

NORTHERN JACANA. *Jacana spinoza*. Fairly common around lakes, streams, and flooded pasture where it hunts in shallow water for fish and insects.

BOAT BILLED HERON. *Cochlearius cochlearius*. Frequents mangroves, marshes, and coastal rivers. Roosts in tree overhanging the water by day, a solitary hunter by night.

YELLOW-THROATED TIGER HERON. *Tigrisoma mexicanum*. Prefers large bodies of water. Common in lowlands but sometimes seen in highland lakes. Stands motionless for long periods waiting for prey to happen by.

PINK FLAMINGO. *Phoenicopterus ruber*. Large numbers congregate during the winter months at Yucatan's Rio Lagartos Reserve. They have been sighted as far south as the Shipstern Nature Reserve in Belize.

ROSEATE SPOONBILL. *Ajala,ajala.* Usually seen feeding in flocks in both fresh and salt water coastal habitats.

BROWN PELICAN. *Pelecanus occidentalis.* Frequents coastal marshes, lagoons, and rivers. Catches fish by plunge-diving from heights up to 10 meters.

YELLOW-CROWNED NIGHT HERON. *Nyctanassa violacea*. Ocean shores and mangrove swamps. Hunts especially for crabs.

WHITE IBIS. *Eudoncimus albus*. Found in both salt and fresh water habitats wherever it can find soft mud in which to probe for food.

In order to study the behaviour of jungle birds without disturbing them, biologists construct a variety of blinds, often high up in the forest canopy.

GREAT EGRET (in breeding plumage). *Casmerodius albus*. The largest of all white herons. Frequents low-elevation lagoons, estuaries, and marshes where it hunts for frogs and fish.

HORNED GUAN. *Oreophasis debianus*. This extremely rare turkey-sized bird inhabits the cloudforests of Chiapas, Mexico, and Guatemala.

OCELLATED TURKEY.*Cyrtonyx ocellatus.*. Fairly common in undisturbed rain forest in northern Guatemala, Belize, and the Yucatan.

JABIRU (immature male). *Jabiru mycteria*. This huge stork, standing nearly as tall as a person, has become very rare. Found in coastal lagoons and marshes where it hunts fish and crustaceans. It roosts and nests in high trees. (Opposite)

GREAT CURASSOW. *Crax rubra*. Male and female performing mating dance. Fairly common in lowland forests up to 1,000 meters. Walks around the forest floor scratching for insects and searching for fruits. Roosts in trees.

PLAIN CHACHALACA. *Ortalis vetula*. Common in lowland forests where they can be seen foraging in groups.

COLLARD ARACARI.
Pteroglossus torquatus. One of three toucans inhabiting the region. They are most common in low-elevation rain forest.

KEEL-BILLED TOUCAN.
Ramphastos sulfuratus. Certainly one of the most beautiful birds of the rain forest, these large toucans can often be seen flying in pairs in the forest canopy.

EMERALD TOUCANET. *Aulacorhynchus prasinus*. Lowlands and mountains.

SCARLET MACAW. *Ara macao*. Endangered

RED-LORED PARROT. *Amazona autumnalis*. Rain forest.

MEALY PARROT. *Amazona farinosa*. Lowlands.

WHITE-FRONTED PARROT. *Amazona albifons*. Lowlands.

MILITARY MACAW. *Ara militaris*. This large macaw has become very rare. Found in lowland forests of southern Mexico.

ELEGANT TROGON. *Trogon elegans.* Low and mid-elevation forests.

THICKET TINAMOU. *Crypturellus cinnameous.* Tropical dry forest.

MONTEZUMA OROPENDOLA. *Psarocolius montezuma.* Common in Caribbean lowlands.

ROYAL FLYCATCHER. *Onychorhynchus coronatus.* Low and mid-elevation forests.

CAPRIMULGUS SALVINI ♂.

WHIPPOORWILL. *Caprimulgus carolinensis.* Breeds in North America. Winters along the Pacific slope of Central America. Strictly nocturnal. (Hand-painted lithographs by John Gould, London, 1838).

ROSE-BELLIED BUNTING. *Passerina rositae.* Breeds in North America. Winter resident of mid-elevation forests.

SNOWY COTINGA. *Carpodectes nitidus.* Caribbean lowlands.

BLACK-COLLARED HAWK. *Burarellus nigricollis*. Low and mid-elevation forests.

ORNATE HAWK-EAGLE. *Spizaetus ornatus.* Low and mid-elevation forests.

SPECTACLED OWL. *Pulsatrix perspicillata*. Lowlands.

STRIPED OWL. *Asio clamator.* Low and mid-elevation forests.

WHITE-EARED HUMMINGBIRD. *Hylocharis leucotis*. Highlands.

COMMON RAVEN. *Corvus corax*. High mountains

HARPY EAGLE. *Harpia harpyia*. The largest eagle in the world inhabits remote rain forest where it hunts for monkeys and sloths.

CRESTED CARACARA. *Polyborus cheriway.* Low and mid-elevation forests.

RED-TAILED HAWK. *Buteo jamaicensis.* Low to upper elevation forests.

MAMMALS

The mammals are a large and diverse group of animals with the particular attribute that the females have special milk-producing glands with which to feed their young. All mammals have hair, warm blood, and a four-chambered heart. They are considered to be the most highly evolved creatures on earth.

Rain forest mammals tend to be largely nocturnal and difficult to see. It is possible, and even likely, to spend long periods of time in jungles where jaguars, ocelots, and kinkajous dwell and never see one. If you are lucky, you may come upon a jaguar's footprint. In some of the large reserves, such as Tikal National Park in Guatemala, it is probable that you will observe howler and spider monkeys, as well as coatimundis. If fortunate, you may spot a grazing brocket deer or a gray-headed tara, a tropical member of the weasel family, running through the shadows. At night, if you shine the beam of a powerful flashlight up into the forest canopy, a bit of patience will yield results. Eventually you will locate the glowing eyes of a kinkajou or ocelot. Often the light causes them to freeze, and the observer has a good opportunity to see them with binoculars. Quite a few large predatory mammals, such as the jaguar, maintain well-defined territories and tend to use the same hunting trails each night. It is possible, by studying their habits, to place a blind in a strategically positioned tree and wait there for the jaguar's arrival after nightfall. The experience of seeing a wild jaguar at close quarters is a thrill not soon forgotten.

Some friends were on an expedition to the ruins of El Mirador in the north of the Maya Biosphere Reserve. One evening, as they sat around the campfire, they heard a crashing sound in the outlying bush. Suddenly a deer ran right through the middle of the camp. In a moment a large jaguar followed in pursuit, immediately disappearing into the darkness. Seconds later all that could be heard was the chirping of crickets. The boys just looked at each other in disbelief and shook their heads. Strange things happen in the jungle!

JAGUAR. *Pantera onca*. This fanciful illustration appeared in Salvin and Godman's monumental work *Biología Centrali Americana* in 1879. The jaguar is truly the king of the jungle. It fears no other creature apart from man. Jaguars exist in two color phases, the more common orange-tan with dark spots and less frequently all black.

CENTRAL AMERICAN WOOLY OPOSSUM. *Caluromys derbianus*. One of several marsupials inhabiting the region. This opossum is omnivorous and largely nocturnal.

CENTRAL AMERICAN CACOMISTLE. *Bassariscus sumichrasti*. Also known as the ringtailed cat or guyanoche, this medium sized carnivore is a member of the family *Procyonidae* along with raccoons and coatimundis.

COATIMUNDI. *Nasua narica*. A member of the raccoon family, these medium-sized diurnal omnivores often travel in troops of 20 or more individuals as they scour the forest floor for roots, insects, and bird eggs.

AGOUTI. *Dasyprocta punctata*. One of the most common rodents in the forest. Diurnal by nature, they are easily seen as they search the forest floor for seeds and fruits.

PACA. *Agouti paca*. Sharing the same habitat with their relatives, the agouti, pacas come out of their dens in the evening while the agouti are retiring. Known as tepezcuintle in Spanish-speaking countries and gibnut in Belize.

KINKAJOU. *Potos flavos*. Equipped with a long prehensile tail, kinkajous are nocturnal and spend the nights foraging in the forest canopy. Omnivorous.

REMAINS OF MASTODON. The skeleton of a mastodon was found when this gentleman was digging a well near the highland town of Huehuetenango, Guatemala. Carbon dated to be some 10,000 years old, the excavation also revealed numerous other animal remains as well as human-made artifacts. The man holds a mastodon molar. In the foreground we see the tusk.

GRISON. *Galictis vittata*. A member of the weasel family *Mustelidae*, grisons resemble small badgers. Strictly carnivorous, they feed on rodents and other small vertebrates.

TAYRA. *Eira barbara*. This two-foot-long mustelid occurs throughout the Neotropics. They are said to hunt in packs and have been known to run down and devour small deer.

RIVER OTTER. *Lutra annectens*. Aquatic mustelids are fairly common in undisturbed riverine habitats. Highly social, they are usually seen in small family groups.

GRAY FOX. *Urocyon cinereoargentus*. Known locally as "gato del monte " for their amazing ability to climb trees. Foxes are among the most adaptable of all mammals and are found in nearly all habitats and even in areas densely inhabited by humans.

TAMANDUA. *Tamandua tetradactyla*. The most common of the three anteaters in Central America (the others are the nearly extinct giant anteater and the tiny silky pigmy anteater). They excavate ant and termite nests with their sharp front claws. Found in the savanna and rain forest.

HOWLER MONKEY. *Alouatta villosa*. Howlers owe their name to the fact that at dawn and dusk males roar, sounding like an enraged jaguar. Traveling through the canopy in troops of ten or more, they feed on tender leaves and shoots.

SPIDER MONKEY. *Ateles geoffroyi*. Known to the Maya as Maxx, spider monkeys can be seen swinging and leaping through the rain forest canopy, playing and searching for succulent fruits and nuts.

FRUIT-EATING BAT. *Artibeus jamaicensis*. Without bats the rain forest as we know it would die. Many tree and plant species depend on them for pollination and seed dispersal. There are more than 150 species in the region.

ARMADILLO. *Dasypus novemcinctus*. Members of the order *Edentata*, along with anteaters and sloths, armadillos are ground dwellers who forage in search of insects and other small prey. When threatened they curl up in a ball protecting themselves with their hard bony skin.

COLLARED PECCARY. *Tayassu tajacu*. The more common of two species of peccary found in Central America, these highly social ungulates are relatively abundant in the undisturbed lowland forests and savannas and can be seen in groups of as many as thirty individuals.

WHITE-LIPPED PECCARY. *Tayassu pecari*. Larger and more dangerous than the collared peccary, these inhabitants of lowland rain forest sometimes can be seen in groups of over one hundred. They have been known to attack humans.

MANATEE. *Trichechus mantus*. These gentle aquatic herbivores have become increasingly surreptitious in order to avoid human hunters. They occur in pockets along the entire Caribbean coast of Central America. They are the largest herbivores in Central America. Mayan fishermen prepared dried manatee meat for a food they called "bucan". With the European invasion of America, many of the pirates and freefooters relied upon bucan as a staple food, and they became known as "buccaneers".

TAPIR. *Tapirus bairdii*. Tapirs are related to rhinoceroses and horses. These gentle vegetarians are hunted extensively and have become very wary and largely nocturnal in their movements.

MARGAY. *Felix weidii*. Smaller and more arboreal than the ocelot, margays are largely nocturnal and feed on insects, small mammals, and birds. Their semi-prehensile tail gives them monkey-like climbing ability, and they are the most arboreal of all the Mesoamerican feline. They are able to leap from limb to limb in incredible feats of acrobatics and are capable of hanging for extended periods using only one hind paw.

BOTTLE-NOSED DOLPHIN. *Tursiops truncatus*. Although usually oceanic, dolphins frequently swim up rivers. In Guatemala these cetaceans have been seen along the western shore of Lake Izabal, more than fifty miles from the sea.

JAGUARUNDI. *Herpailurus yagouroundi*. Its diurnal habits make this small cat the most frequently seen feline in the region. Also known as the little otter cat because its coloration and small head often cause it to be confused with otters.

OCELOT. *Felis pardalis*. Similar in appearance to the margay, these cats can weigh as much as twenty-five pounds. Although excellent tree climbers, they spend much of their time hunting on the forest floor.

BOB CAT. *Lynx rufus*. Reaching the southern limits of its range in the northern mountains of Chiapas, this medium-sized cat is very rare in Central America.

JAGUAR. *Pantera onca*. Large jaguars can weigh up to 400 pounds and reach six feet in length. They are becoming very rare due to the fact that humans like to hunt them for their beautiful skin.

THE HUMAN MOSAIC

Scientists do not agree on the exact date when humans first appeared on Planet Earth. The estimates vary from one to eight to as much as fifteen million years ago, depending on which paleontologist or biochemist is consulted. What scientists do agree on is that all humans have a common ancestry. We all share the same fundamental genetic heritage and derive from the same root lineage. The most recent studies into human genetics and DNA structure eliminate the possibility of there being separate and distinct human races. There is only one human race, *Homo sapiens.* All superficial differences between people, such as color and physical appearance, are due exclusively to environmental adaptations and inbreeding. In the first case, dark pigmentation protects equatorial living humans from excess sun absorption. Inbreeding was the result of separate geographically-dispersed tribes reproducing only among themselves, which compounded particular physical traits. Some millions of years ago, the first humans appeared in Africa or Asia. At some point they began to spread out looking for new territory, possibly stimulated by glacial and interglacial climate changes. These early migrations eventually brought human colonists to every continent. Early seafarers were able to populate even the most remote islands of Oceania and Polynesia, an astounding feat considering their primitive technology.

The earliest record of human presence in Central America dates from approximately 10,000 years. Primitive tools were located around the remains of a mammoth excavated near the town of Huehuetenango, Guatemala. Most scholars believe that these people had come across the Bering Strait before the end of the last Ice Age and slowly worked their way through North America. Whether or not these first people were the direct ancestors of the Maya remains unclear. Some scientists are convinced that certain seafaring people, notably the Vikings, were successfully circumnavigating the globe more than 2,500 years ago and made contact with both coasts of Central and South America. In any event, when Christopher Columbus "discovered" the New World, he was greeted by aboriginal Americans representing cultures which had been flourishing here for millennia. Since then people have arrived to settle in Central America from Europe, Asia, North America, just about

everywhere. It would seem that evolution is intent on bringing us all together again as we were in the beginning.

It is impossible to realistically think about ecology without taking into consideration the human factor. Whether or not there are rain forests in Central America fifty years from now depends completely upon what we humans do today. It is critical that we try harder to put behind us the differences and old grievances which keep us from working together. Time is running out to do what is necessary to protect and preserve the Earth's natural ecology. It is time we wake up to the fact that we are all in one boat, Spaceship Earth. Citizens of the Earth must work cooperatively to protect the healthy functioning of the planet's ecological life-support systems so that human life may continue to survive on this beautiful 8,000-mile-diameter sphere we call home.

Natives of
Central America

NATIONAL PARKS AND WILDLIFE RESERVES

The following is a list of protected natural areas where the visitor may experience tropical forests and habitats. Keep in mind that park development is still in its infancy throughout most of Central America, and many reserves lack modern infrastructure. Well-established reserves, such as Tikal National Park in Guatemala, Monte Cristo National Park in El Salvador, and La Tigra National Park in Honduras, have excellent facilities with visitors' centers, museums, dormitories, and maintained trail systems. More recently established parks, such as the Calakmul Biosphere Reserve in Mexico, Pico Bonito National Park in Honduras, and the Sierra de las Minas Biosphere Reserve in Guatemala, are virtually without any on-site infrastructure, and visitors are encouraged to obtain a guide. The reserves in this list have been included because of their ease of accessibility, diversity of climatic and vegetation types, and their outstanding natural beauty. In the area covered by this book, more than 150 wildlife reserves have already been established. Unfortunately, many of these reserves exist only on paper, and nothing effective is being done to stem the onslaught of illegal logging operations and human colonization. It is my hope that by stimulating responsible ecotourism, more attention will be focused on the plight of these natural areas, and national and international pressure applied to force local governments to uphold their own laws. The loss of our planet's biological diversity due to the destruction of rain forests must be stopped before it is too late. For more complete information concerning all parks and reserves in each country the reader may contact the local authorities.

A few words of advice concerning mosquitoes, vipers, screw worms, guerrillas, dengue fever, and other inconveniences. Most of us who come from a temperate climate have a Hollywood image of a tropical forest with endless swarms of biting and blood-sucking insects. The truth is that the mosquitoes and other biting, stinging creatures are no worse in the jungle than in the northern forests during the summer. One exception would be the case in some coastal swamps which are often plagued with no-see-ums. These tiny, biting insects are small enough to penetrate most types of mosquito netting and seem unaffected by most repellents. One thing that seems to repel the little devils is smoke. Native inhabitants

CERRO CAHUI NATURE RESERVE. This small reserve on the northern edge of Lake Peten-Itza preserves a beautiful section of rain forest.

COCKSCOMB BASIN WILDLIFE SANCTUARY. Southern Belize.

manage to cope by closing themselves up in huts with burning mosquito coils and by smoking cigars, which may not appeal to everyone. In the highland forests, insects are rarely a problem.

Central America is inhabited by a variety of poisonous snakes. The jungle hiker should exercise caution, especially when walking through dense undergrowth. The largest and most dangerous group of poisonous snakes is the pit vipers (sub-family *Crotalinae*). The "pit" refers to small depressions between the eyes and nostrils, which function as heat sensors and aid in the location of prey. Rattlesnakes are pit vipers. Many of these snakes live on the ground, and pose a hazard only if stepped on. The most feared viper in the region is the fer-de-lance (*Bothrops asper*), known in Belize as the "tomigoff" and in the Spanish-speaking countries as the "barba amarilla" (yellow beard) because of its yellow coloring underneath. More deaths are caused by this snake than all the others combined. Most fatalities occur among workers chopping down bush, and most bites occur below the knee indicating that snake-proof leggings could be life savers. The fer-de-lance reach a length of more than seven feet and can be very aggressive if molested. If you happen to see one, which is unlikely, give him a wide berth. In areas where high densities of these vipers are known to exist, such as the Caribbean lowlands, stay on trails whenever possible and avoid walking through dense brush. If you plan to do serious jungle trekking, it would be advisable to buy an anti-venom kit and learn how to use it. Other interesting vipers include the jumping viper (*Bothrops mummifer*), which hurls itself at its perceived attacker, and the eyelash viper (*Bothrops schlegelii*), which comes in two color phases, lovely lime green and lemon yellow. Eyelash vipers, which name comes from the enlarged scales over the eyes, are arboreal and often live in low bushes. Jungle explorers should always be aware of where to put their hands or feet. Don't sit on a log until you have assured yourself that some other creature has not chosen that spot first.

The other main group of poisonous serpents are the coral snakes (family *Elapidae*), which are related to cobras and mambas. The bite of these snakes can be lethal. Because of their habit of living under rocks and logs, they are seldom seen and are not aggressive unless molested. Coral snakes are instantly recognizable by their colored bands although the non-dangerous king snake has very similar appearance. In Belize the natives use a rhyme to remember which one is which, "red and yellow, kill a fellow; red and black, friend of Jack". Most fatalities occur when children pick them up, attracted by their beautiful coloration.

I once knew a young woman who had recently returned from a weeklong expedition into the remote jungles of northern Alta Verapaz Department, Guatemala. After being home for several days she complained about a sore on her derriere which would not heal. I assumed it was a simple infection, cleaned it off with alcohol, and put on a bandage. Several days later the young lady complained that the wound was still stinging. Upon careful examination, I noticed that what appeared to be an infected boil had a small hole in the middle of it. Suddenly something poked its nose out. Screw worm! One day while sunbathing in the jungle, the poor thing had been bitten by a botfly (*Dermatobia hominis*), which had deposited a egg on her skin while sucking blood. The egg had hatched, and the larvae was easily removed. The girl was shook up, but there was no lasting harm. During long field excursions, screw worm can be a problem. Several remedies are prescribed by jungle veterans. One is blocking the breathing hole with Vaseline until the maggot dies of suffocation and then squeeze it out. Another is to do the same with a cloth soaked in tobacco juice. You can also strap a pieced of raw meat over the wound and wait for the larvae to crawl out of its own accord as it is attracted by the smell of the meat. In twenty years of exploring the rain forest, I have not yet been host to a screw worm, but the chance is always there. Remember that there is no real danger involved.

For many years there have been several active guerrilla movements in the region, and visitors may wish to avoid areas of conflict. In remote parts of Guatemala's Peten, Quiche, Huehuetenango, and Alta Verapaz Departments, as well as the Lacandon Jungle in Chiapas, Mexico, wilderness trekkers have a good chance of being stopped by guerrillas and army patrols wanting to know what you are doing there. Generally speaking, there is no problem once they realize that you are a tourist. At times the guerrillas may give you the "opportunity" to make a "contri-bution" to their cause while army troops may confiscate knives or any other equipment. In any case, the best policy is to offer no resistance and do what you are told. Jungle law says that he who has the most guns makes the rules. To avoid such confrontations, it is best to stick to the beaten path in areas where the local people indicate the existence of a problem. Common crime and highway banditry are also part of the Central American scene. It is best to take preventive measures by frequently asking about conditions in the area.

Dr. Bronner wrote that "health is your greatest wealth". Many otherwise good adventures have been ruined or cut short when individuals fall ill. A good dose of prevention and exercising prudence is highly recommended in selecting food and drink. Malaria and dengue fever are common in the lowlands, while amoebic dysentery and giardia are endemic throughout the region. It is recommended to take the antimalarial tablets before, during, and several weeks after leaving the area where the insect is endemic. Avoid being out of doors without the protection of repellents in the evening or whenever the insects are biting. Dengue fever is especially common along the Caribbean coast. Use your bug spray! Unfortunately cholera has also become endemic in the region so eating street food is not recommended in most areas. Seek immediate medical attention if symptoms of high fever and diarrhea persist. Changes in food and water very often cause minor upsets, but by being careful, serious problems can be avoided. Many doctors advise that taking a daily capsule of *Lactobacillus acidofilus* (friendly bacteria naturally occurring in the digestive tract) may help reinforce healthy conditions.

Weather varies from sweltering coastal jungles to freezing ice storms on the exposed tops of volcanoes. For the lowlands, clothing light enough to be comfortable, but tightly woven enough to be bugproof, is essential. In the mountains you will want to prepare for hot sun in the day and cool to cold nights. During the rainy season, May through October, good rainwear and water-proof boots will make the difference between being soggy, cold, and uncomfortable or being warm and happy.

HONDURAS

Honduras is just beginning to open up to ecotourism. With more than 85 national parks and wildlife refuges already established, the country offers an impressive diversity of habitats to be explored by the adventurous travelling naturalist. The best place to obtain general information and orientation concerning ecotourism in Honduras is at the PROLANSATE Foundation office in the port town of Tela. You will find a visitors' center with information and maps covering the entire country.

1. **CELAQUE NATIONAL PARK**. Located about five miles (8 km.) to the west of the provincial capital of Gracias, Lempira Province, the reserve is accessible by dirt road. Celaque is made up primarily of pristine cloud forest and includes the two highest peaks in Honduras, both about 9,200 feet (2,827 m.) high. The word "Celaque" comes from the Aztec meaning "ice waters". Ten rivers of crystal clear, cold water flow from the park and provide water to more than one hundred communities. The 160 square miles (414 sq. km.) protected by the park provide refuge for many endangered species, including jaguar, puma, ocelot, tapir, and the resplendent quetzal. Celaque is considered Honduras' premier cloud forest park.

2. **CUSUCO NATIONAL PARK.** Established in 1959 through the efforts of pioneer Honduras ecologist Hector Fasquelle, the reserve was incorporated into the national park system in 1987. A four-wheel-drive vehicle is recommended for the fifteen-mile (25 km.) drive along an unpaved road running northeast out of Cofradia, Cortez Province. The reserve is primarily made up of cloud forest with interspersed stands of tropical pine species *Pinus patula* and *Pinus maximinoi*. At present fourteen square miles (36 sq. km.) are protected, but there are plans to enlarge the park to include 110 square miles (285 sq. km.).

3. **PICO BONITO NATIONAL PARK**. Pico Bonito (beautiful peak) juts radically up from the coastal plain three miles (5 km.) south of the seaport of La Ceiba, Atlantida Province. Because of sheer cliffs and dense jungle, it is considered the most difficult mountain to climb in all Honduras. As yet, there is little on-site infrastructure, and a guide would be recommended. Two hundred fifty square miles (650 sq. km.) of the wildest jungle and cloud forest await discovery by courageous explorers and naturalists.

4. **CAPIRO-CALENTURA BIOLOGICAL RESERVE.** It is named for the two hills located behind the historic town of Trujillo, Colon Province, the first populated area of the continental Americas. Capiro and Calentura are located at the end of the Nombre de Dios Mountain Range and reach elevations of 2,200 feet (667 m.) and 4,000 feet, (1,235 m.)

respectively. Thirty square miles (78 sq. km.) of tropical rain forest are protected here. Access is by foot from Trujillo. This reserve is especially recommended for bird watchers.

5. LA TIGRA NATIONAL PARK. Located about seven miles (11 km.) northeast, as the crow flies, from Tegucigalpa, the nation's capital, the reserve is reached by paved road through the towns of Rosario or Jutiapa (two separate entrances). In 1958 La Tigra was the first cloud forest reserve to be established in Honduras and boasts well-maintained visitors' centers, a good system of trails, camping area, and courteous forest rangers. Eighty-five square miles (220 sq. km.) of cloud forest and mixed pine-liquidambar forest are included in the reserve. Because of its ease of access, this is one of the country's most popular national parks.

6. PUNTA SAL NATIONAL PARK. Managed by the PROLANSATE Foundation and funded by the United Nations Environmental Program, Punta Sal has been identified as a priority area for sustainable ecotourism development. Located six miles (9 km.) west of the port of Tela, Cortez Province, the reserve can be reached by boat from Tela or by a dirt road to Miami Village and then two hours on foot. The park consists mainly of mangrove swamps and rainforest and includes the only extensive reef system along the continental coast of Honduras. High cliffs tower over pristine salt lagoons where howler monkeys, crocodiles, and otters are easily seen. This is an excellent site for observation of a large variety of shore birds. Three hundred square miles (780 sq. km.) of forest are protected here.

7. LA MURALLA WILDLIFE REFUGE. Located five miles (8 km.) to the north of the town of La Union, Olancho Province, this cloud forest reserve was established to protect the unusually high level of biodiversity found there. Las Parras mountain, within the park, reaches the height of 6,700 feet (2,064 m.). There are well-maintained trails and a visitors' center. Thirty-five square miles (90 sq. km.) of prime quetzal habitat are included in this easily-accessible reserve.

8. CAYOS COCHINOS NATIONAL MARINE PARK. Comprised of thirteen coral islands or cays, the Cayos Cochinos (Pig Islands) have some of the most beautiful reefs for snorkeling and skindiving in all Central America. There are well-preserved mangrove and tropical forests. This is the only habitat on earth where the rare pink boa constrictor is found.

Accommodations are available in the small fishing villages on the islands, where boat tours can also be arranged. You can reach the islands by small plane from the port of La Ceiba or by boat from the town of Nuevo Armenia, Atlantida Province.

9. CUERO Y SALADO WILDLIFE REFUGE. This reserve consists of a system of canals and estuaries formed at the mouths of the Cuero and Salado Rivers and contains intact mangroves, savannahs, and rainforest. It is home to a multitude of marine and terrestrial species, including easily-seen howler, spider, and white-faced monkeys. Almost two hundred species of birds have been identified within the park. The reserve provides refuge to the endangered manatee. It covers an area of eighty square miles (207 sq. km.) and is located 16 miles (27km.) west of La Ceiba, Atlantida Province.

10. RIO PLATANO BIOSPHERE RESERVE. Designed to protect the Platano River and its watershed, this is one of Central America's most important reserves, both because of its size, 3,150 square miles (8,165 sq. km.), and its richness in flora and fauna. Most of the reserve is comprised of virgin rainforest. There are also extensive sandy beaches, mangrove swamps, estuaries, and canal systems at the river's mouth. Numerous unexplored mountains and hills emerge from the jungle. Archaeologists have encounted strange petroglyphs throughout the park, a legacy of an unknown civilization. Legends say that somewhere hidden in the dense jungle are the ruins of the mysterious "white city". There are no roads into this area, which gives an idea of how remote and wild it is. To get into the reserve, you can fly by small plane from La Ceiba to the village of Palacios. From there you must hire a small motorized dug-out canoe or "tuk-tuk" to take you up the river. Accommodations in the area are very primitive so be prepared to rough it. This reserve is highly recommended, but only for the more adventurous traveller.

11. LANCETILLA BOTANICAL GARDENS AND FOREST RESERVE. Located just outside of the port town of Tela, Lancetilla was originally established as an experimental station where exotic species of tropical plants were cultivated and tested for potential commercial and medicinal uses. More than 700 species of plants may be seen in the gardens as well as the largest collection of Asiatic fruit trees in the Western Hemisphere. This includes the durian, which is described as the most delicious but also the worst smelling fruit in the world. The forest reserve in the hills behind the gardens protects the watershed of the Tela River and includes a large area of rain forest.

EL SALVADOR

The smallest and most densely populated country in Central America is finally emerging from the devastation of its decade-long civil war. It seems a miracle that its systems of beautiful and well-maintained nature reserves have survived largely intact. For general information concerning El Salvador's parks and to obtain camping permits, contact the Department of National Parks located in the Ministry of Agriculture in San Salvador.

1. MONTECRISTO NATIONAL PARK. Located eight miles (14 km.) to the northeast of the town of Metapan, Montecristo National Park is El Salvador's portion of the proposed El Trifinio International Biosphere Reserve protecting more than 28,000 acres (11,336 hectares) of cloud forest and mixed pine-oak-liquidambar forest. A diversity of microclimates and habitats gives the area an unusual biological richness containing many endemic species. The international reserve is best accessed from the El Salvador side where there are a visitors' center, botanical garden, and dormitory facilities. A four-wheel-drive vehicle is recommended for the steep ascent along a primitive dirt track. Alternatively, it is possible to walk in from Metapan.

2. CERO VERDE NATIONAL PARK. This park is located 22 miles (37 km.) from the provincial capital of Santa Ana and situated high above Lake Coatepeque. Flanking the perfect cone of Izalco Volcano, this reserve is the most developed in the country with hotel, restaurant, camping facilities, and well-maintained trail systems. The forest is largely mixed pine-oak and provides refuge for a wide variety of wildlife. Marked paths allow you to climb to the summit of Izalco, reaching an elevation of 6,100 feet (1,850 m.).

3. DEININGER WILDLIFE REFUGE. Although small at only 1,600 acres (648 hectares), Deininger is significant because it is the last surviving piece of Pacific coast forest left in all of northern Central America. Cattle ranching, as well as sugar and cotton plantations, have eliminated the once magnificent forests. At Deininger you get a feel of what once was. Spectacular yellow tabebuias, pink sweetpea, golden-yellow buttercup, and huge buttressed silk cotton trees are among the prominent members of the plant community. The towering kapok trees are often festooned with a profusion of epyphytes, purple *Cattleya* orchids, and red and orange bromeliads. There is a visitors' center, botanical garden and well-maintained system of trails. The park is located three miles (5 km.) southeast of the Pacific port town La Libertad.

4. BARRA DE SANTIAGO WILDLIFE REFUGE. Set up to protect a section of the Pacific coastline, this reserve includes beaches, lagoons, and estuary habitats. It is especially important for the preservation of many migratory species who rest here during their north-south seasonal travels. Many shore birds, as well as small mammals, like jaguarundi and otters, find refuge here. The reserve is located three miles (5 km.) southeast of the Guatemalan border.

GUATEMALA

Institutions concerned with reserve management include the Centro de Estudios Conservacionistas (CECON), located at the Botanical Garden, and the Instituto Guatemalteco de Turismo, both in Guatemala City.

1. MAYA BIOSPHERE RESERVE. This enormous reserve of over 3,520,000 acres (1,425,101 hectares), coupled with the adjoining Calakmul Biosphere Reserve in Mexico and the privately-owned and recently expanded Rio Bravo Conservation area in Belize, constitutes the largest protected rain forest in Central America. It is one of the largest and most important tropical forest reserves in the world. Unfortunately, development and management of the reserve have been fraught with problems from the very beginning. Corrupt government officials take payoffs and allow illegal logging operations to continue. Uncontrolled development of the land by poor farmers and cattle ranchers is ignored by the central government. The Maya Biosphere Reserve includes all lands in Guatemala's Peten Department above latitude 17°10´. There are still large sections of totally wild rain forest where few humans ever venture. Expeditions can be organized to trek through the jungle to the ancient Mayan ruins of El Mirador and Agua Azul. As yet there is no infrastructure existing to facilitate tourists. Numerous trails criss-cross the jungle, but there are no maps. It would be best to inquire about conditions in the reserve at the Tikal National Park or at the offices of one of the international conservation organizations in Flores, capital of the Peten Department.

2. TIKAL NATIONAL PARK. Best known as an archaeological reserve, the 126,000 acres (51,012 hectares) of the park are also one of Central America's oldest and largest wildlife preserves. Animals such as jaguar, ocelots, crocodiles, and spider monkeys have been legally protected since 1957. The many miles of maintained trails make Tikal one of the best and most easily-accessed rain forests anywhere. The huge pyramids are ideal bird-watching platforms. There are hotels, museums, camping facilities, and restaurants within the reserve. Because of the exceeding diversity found here and the large size of the park, it is recommended to spend at least a week to get to know the area. Tikal is located forty-three miles (69 km.) to the east of Flores, Peten Department. Busses leave frequently to take you to the park center.

3. BIOTOPO CERRO CAHUI. Located on the northeast edge of Lake Peten Itza, this small reserve of 1,650 acres (668 hectares) is a tropical evergreen forest with epiphyte-encrusted mahogany, ramon, sapodilla, chicle, and giant-buttressed silk cotton trees. The well-maintained trail leads to a lookout on top of Cahui Hill, which has an excellent view of the lake. Many types of palms, ferns, orchids, and philodendrons grow in profusion. The trees are intertwined with lianas, air roots, and strangler figs. Howler and spider monkeys are easy to spot, as are keel-billed toucans, mot-mots, and yellow-breasted trogons. Any bus running between Tikal and Flores can let you off near the entrance to the park. From there it is a two-mile (3 km.) walk to the visitors' center, camping, and lodging.

4. RIO DULCE NATIONAL PARK. The Rio Dulce is an example of what should not happen to a national park. Not too many years ago, this river was wild and a few miles downstream you felt as if you were in the middle of the Amazon. Then came development. Many people built weekend homes along the river, and the international yachting community moved in. The upper portion of the river has become crowded. Nevertheless, Rio Dulce is still worth a visit. In 1976 I began a study of the endangered manatee living in the river with the hope of gaining support to establish a refuge for these gentle aquatic mammals. By 1981 the first manatee reserve was established within the national park, the Biotopo Chocón-Machacas para la Protección del Manatí. It is located in a widening of the Rio Dulce called El Golfete, ten miles (16 km.) up river from the coastal town of Livingston. The boat ride takes you through a spectacular canyon where the wildlife is still abundant. At the manatee reserve are trails, camping facilities and a visitors' center.

5. BIOTOPO DEL QUETZAL. This is one of the most popular reserves because it is easy to get to and the quetzal is the national bird. The park owes its existence to the efforts of pioneer conservationist Mario Dary. He developed the biotopo as a model and prototype for reserve development and environmental education nationwide. Sadly, Dary was assassinated in 1981, but seven of his biotopos remain as testimony to his endeavors to preserve wildlife for all of us. This biotopo protects over 2,500 acres (1,012 hectares) of cloud forest. It is fairly easy to see the quetzal here. The reserve is three hours by car from Guatemala City on the main road to Coban, about two miles (3 km.) before the town of Purulha.

6. LAKE ATITLAN NATIONAL PARK. Located in the Department of Solola, this park is two and one-half hours by car from Guatemala City When you arrive at the lake, considered by many to be the most beautiful in the world, you may wonder where the park is. Unfortunately most of the shoreline has been built up. Still, the lake is impressive in its beauty. For those interested in wildlife it is best to take a boat to Santiago Atitlan or San Pedro, two Indian villages across the lake from Panajachel, the tourist center. From there is it possible to climb any of the three towering volcanoes. The highest is Atitlan, which reaches 11,500 feet (3,531 m). Good cloud forest is found on the Pacific slopes of these volcanoes.

7. PACAYA VOLCANO NATIONAL PARK. Located approximately ten miles (16 km.) south of Guatemala City, Pacaya is the most active volcano in the region and the best place to see spectacular eruptions. At the top are two cones, one active and one quiet. You can climb to the summit of the extinct cone, which is higher than the active one, and look down upon the bubbling and spewing lava. It is best to go with one of the guided groups which leave daily from Antigua.

8. SIERRA DE LAS MINAS BIOSPHERE RESERVE. Established in 1990, this large reserve of 233,000 acres (94,332 hectares) provides protection for a variety of habitats and microclimates. There is cloud forest along the summit of the sierra, mixed pine-oak-liquid ambar forest on the flanks, and dry thorn forest on the Motagua River Valley side. Within the park are some of the wildest mountain forests in Central America where unusually high numbers of unique endemic species are being discovered. This is the home of the harpy eagle, the largest eagle in the world, and the last refuge of the giant anteater. There are two entrance points to the park, one via the village of Chilasco, Baja Verapaz Department, and the other via San Agustin Acasaguastlan, El Progreso Department. A local guide is indispensable to find your way through the reserve.

9. LOS CUCHUMATANES MOUNTAINS NATIONAL PARK (proposed). This high mountain range offers some of the best hiking in the country with spectacular vistas and a brisk alpine climate. The road running from Huehuetenango to San Juan Ixcoy takes you up to an elevation of 11,700 feet (3,600 m.), passsing through pine forests, paramo (alpine shrubland), and beautiful meadows with a profusion of wildflowers, succulents, and agaves. Here mountain lions and ravens share the forest with ocelots and grey-headed taras. The Mam Indian town of Todos Santos is a good place to use as a base during your stay in the mountains.

10. BIOTOPO MONTERRICO-HAWAII. Located twelve miles (20 km.) south of Taxisco, Santa Rosa Department, this park was established to protect extensive mangrove swamps and estuary habitats and provide safe nesting for endangered sea turtles. It is a excellent spot for bird watchers. Large numbers of migratory birds stop here in the winter months. The placid lagoons and canal systems are ideal for viewing aquatic species. There is a visitors' center, turtle hatchery, and trail system.

BELIZE

With less than 200,000 residents, Belize is Central America's least populated nation. Much of the country remains forested. In recent years the idea of promoting ecotourism has taken hold, and national interest has been focused on preserving the natural heritage. The government has established 15 forest reserves over 28 percent of the country. Because of the relative political stability, social tranquillity, and the fact that the people speak English, Belize has become, almost overnight, a mecca for naturalists interested in tropical ecosystems. One of the best places to obtain general information on reserves and to meet some dedicated, idealistic conservationists is at the Monkey Bay Wildlife Sanctuary and Education Center. Monkey Bay is located at mile 32 (51 km.) on the Western Highway which runs between Belize City and the capital of Belmopan.

1. CHAN CHICH/GALLON JUG NATURE RESERVE. Widely considered to be the best managed and well-protected reserve in Belize, Chan Chich may be one of the best places in the world to catch a glimpse of a wild jaguar. Five species of felines are protected in the reserves. Two large lagoons provide refuge for aquatic bird species. From my experience, the reserve has a high density of fer-de-lance so watch where you put your feet. Other creatures you may see include monkeys, coatis, tapir, and more than 250 species of birds. Chan Chich is privately owned and managed by pioneer Belizean conservationist Barry Bowen. It is two and one-half hours by car from the town of Orange Walk.

2. HALF MOON CAY NATURAL MONUMENT. The first reserve to be established under the National Parks System Act of 1981, Half Moon Cay is in the southeast corner of Lighthouse Reef, some fifty miles (80 km.) southeast of Belize City. Thousands of sea birds nest on the cay, including the red-footed booby and the magnificent frigatebird. Ospreys, mangrove warblers, and iguanas are commonly seen. Seventy-seven migratory bird species have been recorded here. Lighthouse Reef is known as one of the world's finest dive locations. It is here where you find the famous "blue hole", a fantastically beautiful submarine cave. Excursions to Lighthouse Reef may be arranged in Belize City or Cay Caulker.

3. HOL CHAN MARINE RESERVE. Established in 1987 to protect 3,000 acres (1,215 hectares) of coral reef habitat, Hol Chan is the ideal place for snorkeling. Coral reefs are the marine equivalent of rain forests with respect to diversity of species. Spotted eels, butterfly fish, tiger groupers, and the occasional squadron of barracuda may be seen swimming among the beautiful coral formations. The reserve is located midway between Ambergris and Caulker Cays.

4. COMMUNITY BABOON SANCTUARY. Established in 1985 to protect a large black howler monkey population, this reserve is unique in that it is managed by volunteers and private landowners as a cooperative venture among seven villages in central Belize. The eighteen-square-mile (47 sq. km.) sanctuary on the Belize River seeks to preserve a beautiful section of riparian forest which provides refuge for some 200 kinds of birds, anteaters, deer, coati, peccary, and many other species. A visitors' center and small museum are located in the town of Bermuda Landing, approximately twenty-five miles (40 kms.) northwest of Belize City.

5. SHIPSTERN NATURE RESERVE. Located in Corozal District, the Shipstern Nature Reserve is 19,800 acres (8,016 hectares) of hardwood forests, mangrove swamps, and saline lagoon systems, as well as wide belts of savannah. Saline mudflats are punctuated by isolated hillocks of limestone, planted with palms and hardwoods. Two hundred species of birds, sixty species of reptiles, and close to 200 species of butterflies can be seen. Jaguar, ocelot, tapir, and brocket deer are among the reserve's mammalian residents. It is a one-hour drive from Orange Walk to the reserve visitors' center.

6. COCKSCOMB BASIN WILDLIFE SANCTUARY. Located in south central Belize near the town of Maya Center, this reserve was established in 1984 and expanded in 1990 to include more than 100,000 acres (40,500 hectares) of rain forest. The Cockscomb Basin, ringed on three sides by high ridges and mountains, rises from about 300 feet (92 m.) above sea level to 3,675 feet (1,130 m.) at the summit of Victoria Peak. The area has the highest density of jaguars yet recorded. A visitors' center, camping and dormitory facilities, and an excellent system of trails should put this reserve on your priority list.

7. CROOKED TREE WILDLIFE SANCTUARY. Situated midway between Belize City and Orange Walk and three miles west of the Northern Highway lies the little farming and fishing village of Crooked Tree. In 1984 the Belize Audubon Society was successful in establishing a 3,200 acre (1,296 hectares) reserve surrounding the village. Huge numbers of migratory birds flock to the rivers, swamps and lagoons each year during the winter. The sanctuary hosts a small population of rare jabaru storks, one of the largest in the world with a ten-foot wing span.

The best way to see the area is to hire a boat at the village for a tour of the lagoons. There is a visitors' center ecological exhibit at the reserve's headquarters.

8. RIO BRAVO CONSERVATION AREA. Established by the Program for Belize in 1987, this 150,000 acre (60,729 hectares) reserve in northwestern Belize is dedicated to wildlife conservation, biological and archaeological research, sustainable forestry and agriculture, and natural history tourism. The Program is funded largely by the Massachusetts Audubon Society in cooperation with its Belizean counterpart. The land is covered in tropical evergreen forest and contains lagoons populated with the endangered Morellet's crocodiles, crystal-clear streams, ancient Mayan ruins, and dense jungle. An unpaved all-weather road takes you from Orange Walk to the park headquartes.

9. MOUNTAIN PINE RIDGE FOREST RESERVE. Nearly 500 square miles (1,295 sq. km.) of forest are included in this reserve, which is southeast of San Ignacio. Most of the northern portion of the park is reforested pine and is not particularly rich in species. Nevertheless, it is a beautiful area to visit. Especially popular are the Rio On waterfalls for a cool swim and the spectacular Hidden Valley Falls which plunge nearly 1,625 feet (500 m.) into the misty valley below. The Rio Frio Caves near the Augustine logging camp are also worth a visit. Pine forest gives way to rain forest in the southern portion of the reserves. Here are also the ruins of Caracol, one of the greatest ancient Mayan cities. Access to the reserve is via a deeply-rutted track running out of the town of Santa Elena, Cayo District. Numerous ecotourism establishments in the area offer horseback trips, rafting, and jungle expeditions.

10. GUANACASTE NATIONAL PARK. This park is at the junction of the Western and Hummingbird Highways, three miles (5 km.) east of Belmopan, where the Roaring Creek and Belize River meet. It is worth a stop on your tour of Belize if only to see the one giant guanacaste tree which somehow survived the loggers. The tree is truly inmense and covered with an amazing variety of epiphytes, ferns, and orchids. A well-maintained trail system runs through the park, and there are excellent spots to take a swim. A visitors' center and small museum are located at the entrance.

MEXICO

For general orientation and the opportunity to meet the people involved with parks development in southern Mexico, I would recommend paying a visit to the Instituto de Historia Natural located in the zoological park, ZOOMAT, in Tuxtla Gutierrez, the capital of Chiapas State. The private organization PRONATURA is also active throughout the region and has offices in San Cristobal de las Casas, Chiapas, and Merida, Yucatan.

1. LAGUNA XELHA NATIONAL PARK. This beautiful, clear lagoon is the ideal place for those who are not certified divers to see the rainbow-hued tropical marine fauna with snorkeling equipment. A truly amazing variety of fish can be seen here. This park is located in Quintana Roo State seven miles (12 km.) north of Tulum. Arrive early as it tends to get crowded. It is best to bring your own snorkeling gear although the park does rent equipment.

2. RIO LAGARTOS SPECIAL BIOSPHERE RESERVE. Located on the northern edge of the Yucatan Peninsula, this reserve is probably best known for its large population of pink flamingos. Salt marshes and lagoons, mangrove swamps, and dune ecologies predominate. Birding is excellent. To see the flamingos and fully appreciate the reserve, it is necessary to hire a boat at the town of Rio Lagartos. Cancun is several hours away by car.

3. SIAN KA'AN BIOSPHERE RESERVE. This huge reserve of 1,161,600 acres (470,283 hectares) includes extensive tracts of pristine mangroves and tropical evergreen forest, as well as innumerable lagoons, canals, reefs and coconut palm-fringed beaches. The entrance and ranger station are located just south of Tulum. From here a dirt track runs some eighteen miles (30 km.) into the reserve. Along the way there are excellent locations for camping and hiking. Boats and guides can be hired at the town of Punta Allen at the end of the road.

4. CALAKMUL BIOSPHERE RESERVE. Located in the State of Campeche, the reserve is accessed by a dirt track running south from the town of Xpujul where guides can be hired. This enormous park is made up of a vast sea of tropical evergreen forest extending as far as the eye can see. Drier and lower than the rain forests, located farther south, the vegetation is very dense and impossible to get through without a machete. Deep in the reserve lies the ruins of a major Mayan city under nearly completely overgrown jungle.

5. EL TRIUNFO BIOSPHERE RESERVE. Established in 1972 through the efforts of pioneer Mexican conservationist Professor Miguel Alvarez del Toro, El Triunfo was designated as a Biosphere Reserve by federal decree in 1990 and expanded to include a total of 265,000 acres (107,290 hectares). Due to marked geological, climatic, and topological variations, El Triunfo presents a great diversity of floristic zones. It includes ten distinct habitats, from cloud forest and paramo along the crest of the Sierra Madre, to pine-oak-liquidambar forest on the slopes and rain forest at lower elevations. Beautiful riparian forests are found in numerous river valleys. The reserve provides refuge for many endangered species, including the resplendent quetzal and horned guan. There is a good system of trails, camping area, and dormitory at the research station. Located in the southwest corner of Chiapas, it is necessary to obtain a permit from the Instituto de Historia Natural in Tuxtla Gutierrez in order to visit the reserve.

6. MONTES AZULES BIOSPHERE RESERVE. Established in 1978 to protect the pristine wilderness of the Lacandon jungle, Montes Azules covers an area of more than 725,000 acres (293,522 hectares). The vegetation consists of exuberant tropical rain forest typified by the great diversity of tree species, among them chicozapote, ramon, silk cotton, and guarumbo. The canopy is about 100 feet (30 m.) above the floor, and numerous trees reach heights of over 180 feet (55 m.). Many rare and endangered species thrive here, including harpy eagles, macaws, jaguar, and howler monkeys. Deep in the reserve are the turquoise-blue, crystal-clear waters of Laguna Miramar. There is a superb campsite for jungle explorers. As yet the area is very wild, access is difficult, and visitors' facilities are nonexistent. Contact the Instituto de Historia Natural in Tuxtla Gutierrez for further information concerning visiting the reserve.

7. SUMIDERO CANYON NATIONAL PARK. A huge canyon was created over the eons by Grijalva River, the depth of which reaches nearly 5,000 feet (1,500 m.). Low, dense jungle covers much of the 50,000 acres (20,243 hectares) within the park. Boat rides through the canyon can be arranged at the town of Chiapa de Corzo. A road out of Tuxtla Gutierrez takes you to a spectacular overlook, from which there is a trail through the jungle leading to a cave.

8. LAGUNAS DE MONTEBELLO NATIONAL PARK. This park was created to protect the natural integrity of sixty beautiful lagoons of distinct sizes and colors. More than 13,200 acres (5,344 hectares) of cloud forest and pine-oak-liquidambar forest cover the undulating hills. Many orchids, bromeliads, and other epiphytes are present. Quetzales can be seen flying through the canopy. It is located twenty-five miles (40 km.) east of the town of Trinitaria.

9. LA ENCRUCIJADA ECOLOGICAL RESERVE. Located along the Pacific coast in the southeast sector of Chiapas State, La Encrucijada includes mangrove swamps, brackish and salt lagoons, canals, and beaches. The reserve extends from Chocohuital Estuary near Pijijiapan in the north to Cabildos Lagoon in the south, covering nearly ninety miles (150 km.) of coastline. It is an extremely important refuge for aquatic and migratory birds. To get to the park, take the unpaved road which heads southwest from the town of Esquintla. Eighteen miles (30 km.) down the road is the fishing village of Las Garzas. From here you can hire a boat to take you to the reserve headquarters at La Concepción where it is possible to camp.

10. EL OCOTE FOREST RESERVE. Located in the northern mountains of Chiapas, this 110,000 acre (44,535 hectares) reserve conserves three distinct types of tropical evergreen forest. Huge cedar trees, silk cottons, ramons, and zapotes tower among palms of many varieties. Refuge is provided to large numbers of endangered animal species, inluding tapir, mountain lion, spider monkeys, jaguar, and harpy eagles. The reserve is situated thirty miles (50 km.) northwest of Tuxtla Gutierrez. It is best to get exact directions and camping permits at the offices of the Instituto de Historia Natural in Tuxtla.

11. LAGUNA BELGICA EDUCATIONAL PARK. This small park of about 100 acres (40 hectares) is located about two hours by car north of Tuxtla Gutierrez. Within its area is a little lagoon, a swamp, pine-oak-liquidambar forest and evergreen forest. In the spring this is a good place to see the gaudy leaf frog with its bright green coloration and bulging red eyes. There is an orchid garden with various rare species. Camping is possible by obtaining a permit at the Instituto de Historia Natural in Tuxtla.

THE EMBASSY OF NATURE

The Embassy of Nature (Embajada del Reino Natural) was founded by individuals feeling an urgent need to participate actively in the defense of the rivers, forests, lakes, and jungles that we love. The organization is comprised of a circle of friends from around the planet. It is our belief that the present greed and ignorance motivated destruction of Earth's ecological life support system is placing all humans in peril of extinction. We must act now!

Our fundamental orientation is one of love and respect for all life. We believe that every creature, big and small, is sacred. All deserve to be able to pursue their unique paths without unnecessary interference. Science and development without heart inevitably becomes hellish. If humans are to continue on Planet Earth, we must embrace a new philosophy of life which includes greater respect for all beings, including the non-human ones.

Effective environmental education is crucial and is aimed at stimulating people to become actively involved in the defense of the natural ecology. Our organization is dedicated to producing green educational materials to use in schools and impact the public at large. We cannot wait for scientific and governmental bureaucracies to lead us out of our planetary crisis. We must do it ourselves.

Recommended Reading

Alvarez del Toro, M. *Las Aves de Chiapas*. Tuxtla Gutierrez, Chiapas, Mexico: Instituto de Historia Natural, 1980.

--------------. *Los Reptiles de Chiapas*. Tuxtla Gutierrez, Chiapas, Mexico: Instituto de Historia Natural, 1983.

--------------. *Los Mamíferos de Chiapas*. Chiapas, Mexico: Gobierno del Estado, 1991.

--------------. *Chiapas y Su Biodiversidad*. Chiapas, Mexico: Gobierno del Estado, 1993.

Caufield, C. *In the Rainforest*. Chicago, IL: University of Chicago Press, 1984.

Coe, Michael D. *The Maya*. New York, NY: Thames and Hudson, 1980.

Davis, L.I. *A Field Guide to the Birds of Mexico and Central America*. Austin, TX: University of Texas, 1972.

Edwards, E.P. *A Field Guide to the Birds of Mexico*. Sweet Briar, VA: E.P. Edwards.

Forsyth, A. and K. Miyata. *Tropical Nature*. New York, NY: Scribner, 1984.

Fuller, R. Buckminster. *Critical Path*. New York, NY: St. Martin's Press, 1981.

Hall, E.R. *The Mammals of North America*. New York, NY: John Wiley & Sons, 1981.

Holdridge, C. *Life Zone Ecology*. San Jose, Costa Rica: Tropical Science Center Publications, 1967.

Jacobs, M. *The Tropical Rain Forest: A First Encounter*. New York, NY: Springer-Verlag, 1988.

Janson, Thor. *Animales de Centroamerica en Peligro*. Guatemala City, Guatemala: Editorial Piedra Santa,1981.

--------------. *Quetzal*. Guatemala City, Guatemala: Editorial Artemis, 1992.

--------------. *In the Land of Green Lightning: The World of the Maya*. Rohnert Park, CA: Pomegranate Publications, 1994.

Kricher, J.C. *A Neotropical Companion*. Princeton, NJ: Princeton University Press, 1989.

Leopold, A.S. *Wildlife of Mexico*. Berkeley, CA: University of California Press. 1959.

Lovelock, J. *Healing Gaia: Practical Medicine for the Planet*. New York, NY: Harmony Books, 1991.

Myers, N. *The Primary Source: Tropical Forests and Our Future*. New York, NY: W.W. Norton, 1984.

Perry, D. Life *Above the Jungle Floor*. New York, NY: Simon & Schuster, 1986.

Peterson, Roger Tory and E.L. Calif. *A Field Guide to Mexican Birds*. Boston, MA: Houghton Mifflin Co., 1973.

Skutch, Alexander F. *A Bird Watcher's Adventures in Tropical America*. Austin, TX: University of Texas Press, 1977.

Tedlock, Dennis. *Popol Vuh*. New York, NY: Simon & Schuster, 1985.

Wilson, E.O., editor. *Biodiversity*. Washington D.C.: National Academy Press, 1989.